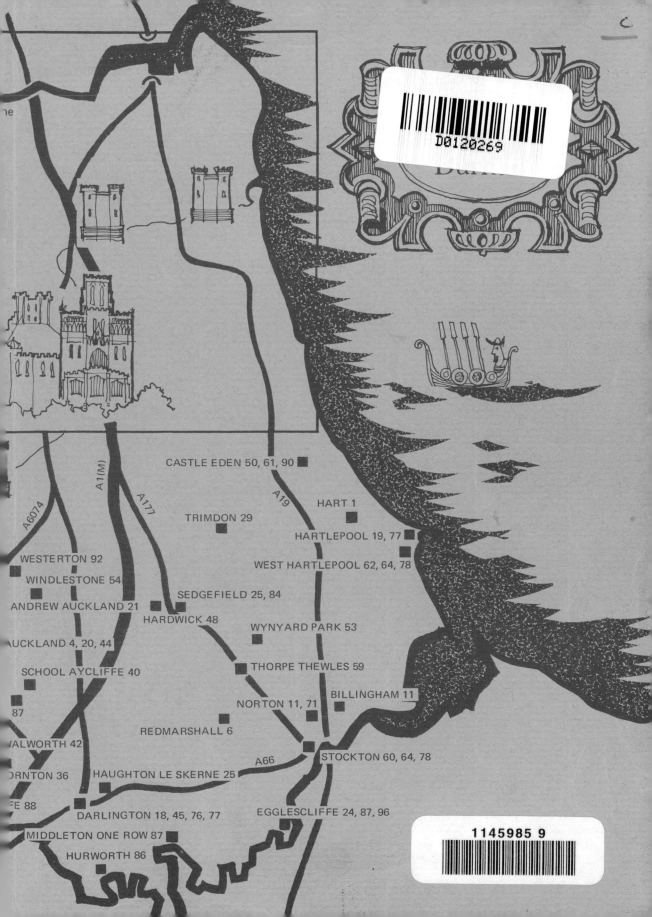

CASTLE EDEN 50, 61, 90

HART 1

A19

TRIMDON 29

HARTLEPOOL 19, 77

WESTERTON 92

WEST HARTLEPOOL 62, 64, 78

WINDLESTONE 54

SEDGEFIELD 25, 84

ANDREW AUCKLAND 21

HARDWICK 48

WYNYARD PARK 53

UCKLAND 4, 20, 44

THORPE THEWLES 59

SCHOOL AYCLIFFE 40

BILLINGHAM 11

NORTON 11, 71

87

REDMARSHALL 6

ALWORTH 42

STOCKTON 60, 64, 78

A66

ORNTON 36

HAUGHTON LE SKERNE 25

FE 88

DARLINGTON 18, 45, 76, 77

EGGLESCLIFFE 24, 87, 96

MIDDLETON ONE ROW 87

HURWORTH 86

A1(M)

A177

A6074

HISTORIC ARCHITECTURE
of
COUNTY DURHAM

Hart, St. Mary,
15th-century font

Historic Architecture of COUNTY DURHAM

by
Neville Whittaker MA, ARIBA
and
Ursula Clark

Sponsored by
THE CIVIC TRUST FOR THE NORTH EAST
and
DURHAM COUNTY COUNCIL

Oriel Press

© The Civic Trust for the North East 1971
First published 1971

ISBN O 85362 129 2
Library of Congress Catalogue Card No. 77-160364

The Durham stone masons craft — St. Helen's Hall, Auckland

Frontispiece. Durham, the Norman Chapel in the Castle c.1070
Title Page. Sunderland, Holy Trinity, early 18th century font

ACKNOWLEDGEMENTS

A general thank you is extended to all those whose patience and encouragement have made this book possible as, individually, they would have made a very long list. In particular, the Editors wish to thank owners and custodians of properties who have allowed access for photography—often at strange hours and on repeated occasions.

Especial thanks are extended to Ian R. J. Woods for his advice, to Rosemary Whittaker, Peter Chatfield and Bruce Allsopp for their careful reading of text, their comments and helpful criticism, and to Joyce M. Clark for her untiring patience at a typewriter.

Photographic Credits:-
South Shields Corporation, page 6 (Roman tombstone)
Ursula Clark — all other photographs

Published by
ORIEL PRESS LIMITED
32 Ridley Place, Newcastle upon Tyne, NE1 8LH
Text set by City Engraving Co. (Hull) Ltd.
Printed at the Country Press by Lund Humphries & Co. Ltd., Bradford

Preface

This book is not a history of architecture. It sets out first to be a record and appreciation of some of those buildings which, by their architectural merit, their place in the history of the county or contribution to the scene and its character, are part of the nature of Durham. The second aim is to reveal and increase understanding of the buildings we illustrate and the many others for which there simply is not space.

In an age of increasing internationalism in architecture and the general fabric of our lives, individuality and a sense of identity and place are precious. Historic buildings relate us to our past and to the rich culture of the north of England which is revealed, not only in castles and cathedrals, but also in vernacular architecture.

For centuries Durham was a quiet and relatively backward agricultural and pastoral district with deep valleys leading up from a fine coastline into the hills. In sheltered places landowners built their spacious mansions and the country became studded with handsome farmhouses, seemly cottages, small market towns and villages. In the western hills, lead mining flourished and packhorses carried the ore to various places for smelting. Then, with the Industrial Revolution, coal and iron became important and the county was exploited and despoiled, much of the wealth earned from its labour and its minerals going to landlords who increasingly preferred to live elsewhere. A blight of cheap, ephemeral development settled upon many of the once beautiful places and throughout the eastern part of the county we are now aware of two civilisations (if that is the word), one based upon a rural economy, the other upon industry. With the decay of mining there was a legacy of dereliction which sometimes blinds even the most discerning critics to the very real and enduring beauties of County Durham.

The presence of Durham City, at the heart of the county, containing buildings of superb quality, of international importance, and of outstanding drama, tends to distract attention from the architectural quality of the rest of the county and, for this reason, only a few pages are given to the City so that the architectural wealth of the whole County may be fairly represented.

Architecture in the county of Durham really began with the Roman conquest in the first century A.D. Between then and the departure of the Romans in the fifth century, it was an area of primitive settlement, traversed by lines of communication with the northern frontier. Along these were staging posts, sometimes fortified, and occasional villa settlements, as at Old Durham, east of the present city. The main Roman sites are Binchester, Ebchester, Piercebridge, Lanchester and South Shields — the only one at present open to visitors.

With the departure of the Romans, two centuries of barbarism followed. Celtic Christianity came from Iona to a new nucleus at Lindisfarne in the seventh century and under St. Wilfrid's guidance was reconciled with Roman Christianity — coming from the south — at the Synod of Whitby in 664. The principal centres of early Christianity in Durham were at Jarrow and Monkwearmouth. Viking raids, followed by the Danish conquest in the ninth century, quenched the light of Northumbrian civilisation and according to legend, the fugitive monks of Lindisfarne, in 995, brought the body of their last Bishop, St. Cuthbert, to the present site of Durham Cathedral, where it now rests behind the high altar.

In 1066, King Harold of England was in the north fighting off fresh invaders from Scandinavia when news of William's expedition sent him hurrying south to be defeated at Hastings. Following the Northumbrian revolt in 1069 a Norman castle was built at Durham and the Prince Bishops, as rulers of the Palatinate, wielded almost regal powers with their own army, courts and coinage. The Palatinate derived originally from the grant of land by Ecgfrith to St. Cuthbert. Its powers were gradually pruned and finally ended in 1836.

Above. South Shields, Roman tombstor
Below. Redmarshall, St. Cuthbert, an amalgam of styles and periods

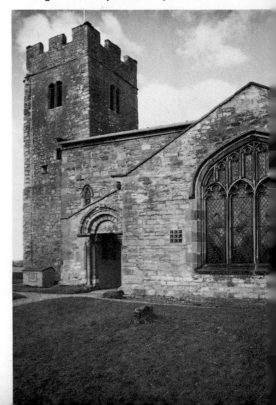

Introduction

West Auckland, 17th-century manor

Though Newcastle on the River Tyne was a substantial barrier against Scottish raids, County Durham was by no means immune and it was not until the union of the crowns in 1603 that more settled conditions permitted the development of manor houses and better farming methods. Even then, progress was relatively slow and the great age of agrarian development, with its fine houses and landscaped parks, did not come until the eighteenth century.

With growing prosperity, the towns were furnished with elegant Georgian houses and most of the farmhouses and cottages were rebuilt. The genius and ideas of Capability Brown, who was born in neighbouring Northumberland, were particularly congenial to the rolling landscape of much of County Durham and though the moors and dales to the west retain their austere character, the more fertile parts became a succession of landscaped parks from Raby near the Tees to Gibside where the Derwent flows into the Tyne.

The following century saw this gentle, agricultural economy change swiftly and devastatingly with the increasing search for the county's vast mineral wealth.

County Durham is an area of great contrasts. It contains some of the most superb architecture in Western Europe. It also contains landscape sharply contrasted between genial lowland areas of fine villages and manors, uplands of moorland and forest with scattered farms and cottages, and large towns containing some of the best and worst products of nineteenth century urbanism.

Sunderland, Monkwearmouth Station 1848, designed by Thomas Moor of Bishopwearmouth. It was erected by the 'Railway King', George Hudson while he was Parliamentary Member for the town.

Anglo-Saxon architecture is part of the great Romanesque tradition which evolved in Western Europe after the fall of the Roman Empire. Northumbria in the seventh and eighth centuries was a light to the world and its surviving architecture in Durham and Northumberland shows a standard of design and structural achievement which, north of the Alps, had few contemporary rivals.

Churches were generally long and high with remarkably slender walls. Though round ends were known, the general practice in the Celtic church was to build a square end and it is an interesting fact that this became a distinguishing characteristic of English churches throughout the Middle Ages and led to the development of the great east window which is the glory of many of our cathedrals. Roofs were of steep pitch and there were narrow openings set high in the walls. Arches were used but sometimes they were cut out of a single stone (arched lintels) and at Jarrow can be seen two canted stones forming a pointed 'arch' which is often thought to be a characteristic of Anglo-Saxon architecture, though it is rare and also occurs in France and Germany.

Monkwearmouth, St. Peter
Left. The 9th century tower porch and sculptured sepulchral cross

Below. Jarrow, St. Paul, Saxon masonry and windows

ANGLO-SAXON   JARROW, St. Paul

Above. The tower, probably rebuilt by Prior Aldwin c.1075
Below. Gable-headed doorway

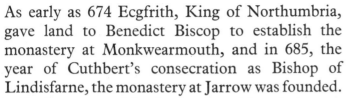

The chancel was built by Ceolfrid, the first Abbot.
Above the arch is the dedication tablet

As early as 674 Ecgfrith, King of Northumbria, gave land to Benedict Biscop to establish the monastery at Monkwearmouth, and in 685, the year of Cuthbert's consecration as Bishop of Lindisfarne, the monastery at Jarrow was founded.

Both communities have close historical associations with Bede, a pupil of Benedict Biscop. Both were sacked by Danish invaders, but the churches fortunately survived together with substantial traces of the monastic buildings. At Jarrow, the chancel—originally the nave—has walls of particularly fine, well-finished masonry.

Illingham, St. Cuthbert, tower, post 1040

eaham, St. Mary, probably early Norman

Norton, St. Mary, plain Saxon arch in the crossing c.1020

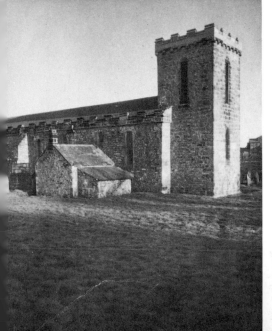

Escomb is the least altered Anglo-Saxon church in the north of England. Except for the early Gothic lancets, the nineteenth century windows and the roof, the surviving fabric is almost untouched. The original windows remain as small round-headed openings high in the walls. (Recent excavation has indicated that the original plan was more complex).

With the Norman Conquest and swift growth in the power of the Palatinate, many Saxon churches such as St. Mary Seaham, and Norton (the only northern cruciform Saxon church) were enlarged in the new style and techniques of construction introduced in the building of Durham Cathedral.

Romanesque Churches

DURHAM CATHEDRAL

Durham Cathedral is one of the great architectural experiences of Europe. As the shrine of St. Cuthbert, it was the culmination of four hundred and fifty years of early Christianity in the north of England. With the exception of the Chapel of the Nine Altars and the fifteenth century stages of the tower, the main structure remains substantially a building of 1093-1140.

Apart from its siting, mass and scale, it is important historically for the technical innovations and experiments it embodies.

Here is some of the earliest rib vaulting in Europe — a form of vaulting lighter and more elegant than the tunnel and groin vaults then in use. Durham Cathedral is not only a superb culmination of Romanesque architecture; it pioneered the Gothic style which depended upon the separation of rib and panel in vaulting. The mass, power and confidence of the nave leads on to the lighter, more decorative Chapel of the Nine Altars. The massive nave columns and rich geometric detail give way to clusters of small columns — some of grey Frosterley marble from Weardale — and more naturalised ornament.

The Galilee Chapel at the west end is a late flourish of Romanesque architecture; light, almost flimsy, in comparison with the earlier work. The ornament and decorations are elegant; the 'water leaf' capitals are a graceful development of earlier capitals, although the forcefulness of the early work is still seen in the zig-zag decoration on the arcading. The tomb of the Venerable Bede is here.

Galilee or Lady Chapel, 1157-1195

Right. Chapel of the Nine Altars, 13th-century Gothic vaulting

Left. Lierne vault of the central tower 1465 by master mason Thomas Barton, seen rising above the Norman crossing. Compare with the ribbed vault of 1099-1110

Above. Pittington, St. Lawrence, arcading c.1165 inserted into the Saxon church. Note 12th-century wall paintings

Above left. Church Kelloe, St. Helen, late Norman cross

Left. Sherburn Hospital, the Chapel founded 1181 and rebuilt in 1868 by Austin and Johnson of Newcastle

Early Norman architecture is typified by the increased use of round-headed arches, ribbed vaults, massive masonry and sparse ornament, generally of geometric pattern. The rich decoration of formal and natural motifs came later and reached its climax in the Galilee Chapel of the Cathedral. The team of craftsmen under Bishop Pudsey's supervision which built the Chapel, later rebuilt and extended the small Saxon church at Pittington in the same manner.

Above. Lanchester, All Saints, the tympanum—
probably 13th century

Above right. Interior view west showing Norman
~~arch~~ and nave. The columns are probably Roman
~~shafts~~ re-used

Right. Edmondbyers, St. Edmund, 12th century,
rebuilt 1858

Below. Trimdon, St. Mary, Norman church restored
~~in~~ the 19th century. It is attractively set on a spacious
~~village~~ green

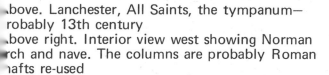

Above. Vault of the Prior's Kitchen 1366-1370 designed by John Lewyn

Left. Vaulting in the Dormitory Undercroft, 13th century

County Durham was dominated by the power of the Benedictine Prior of Durham whose influence precluded the establishment of other monasteries.

Finchale Priory, in a sheltered bend of the Wear valley, was a cell of Durham. The Priory was founded on the site of the small church of St. Godric, shortly after his death in 1170, and building began in earnest in 1196, but the remains are substantially those of a thirteenth century Benedictine House.

In contrast, the parent house at Durham was sited with the Castle on the peninsula above the Wear. After the dissolution of the monasteries some of the buildings were converted to other uses but they remain to this day one of the most complete and impressive groups of monastic buildings in Britain. Especially interesting is the vaulted structure of the Prior's Kitchen.

Left. Dormitory Roof 1398-1404

FINCHALE PRIORY
Frater House, 14th century

DARLINGTON, St. Cuthbert

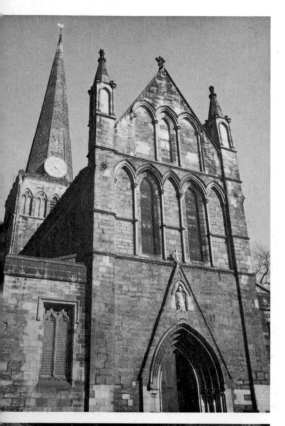

Gothic architecture became established in Durham in the thirteenth century and the finest and largest churches date from that period: Houghton-le-Spring, Darlington, Easington and the most splendid of them all, St. Hilda at Hartlepool. The northern counties produced an 'Early English' architecture of their own, typified by elongated lancet windows, often in groups of three or five, forming the main feature of the square east end of the churches. Examples survive at Easington, Ryton (renewed in 1844), Gainford, Medomsley, Lanchester and Cockfield.

Churches like Easington and Houghton-le-Spring are wide, spacious and simple. Tracery and decoration are severe and towers are usually squat and solid although there are notable exceptions like St. Andrew Auckland. Spires are rare (pp. 22,23).

From the end of the thirteenth century little church building took place. What work did go on was generally limited to the elaboration, extension and decoration of existing buildings including window tracery at Houghton-le-Spring, Sedgefield and the great west and south windows of Durham Cathedral. The tower at Sedgefield was constructed in the fifteenth century; as was the addition of a final topping stage to the central tower of the Cathedral — a remarkable example of northern genius, at once transforming the long horizontal mass of the Romanesque building into a lofty Gothic form.

Above left. West front showing Gothic arcading and lancets, 13th century. The spire was rebuilt in 1752

Left. Interior of transept. The church is almost wholly of the first half of the 13th century

Gothic Churches

HARTLEPOOL, St. Hilda

Above. Tower and great buttresses of the west end, c.1250

Left. Interior looking east, showing the nave and chancel arch c. 1200 and the baluster shaped font of 1728, the gift of George Bowes. The church was originally intended to be completed with western transepts around the tower. It was sensitively restored by W. D. Caroe between 1925 and 1932

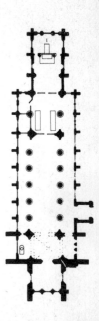

Right. Plan of church

Easington, St. Mary, 12th-century tower and 13th-century interior. Woodwork see pages 24,25

Stanhope, St. Thomas c.1210

Auckland, St. Helen, late 12th and 13th-century chu

Gothic Churches

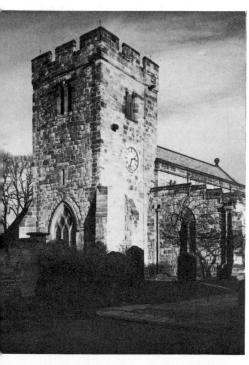

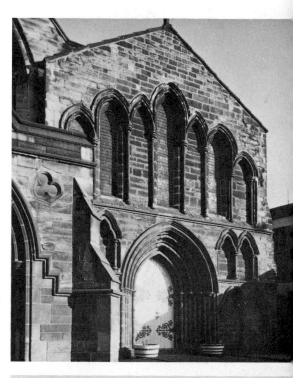

Left.
Whickham,
St. Mary

Right.
Gateshead,
Holy Trinity
—formerly
St. Edmund's
Chapel

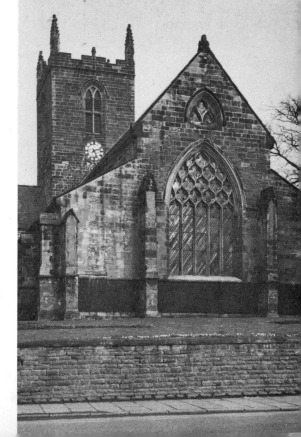

Left.
Auckland,
St. Andrew

Right.
Houghton le
Spring, St.
Michael.
Tracery
c.1350

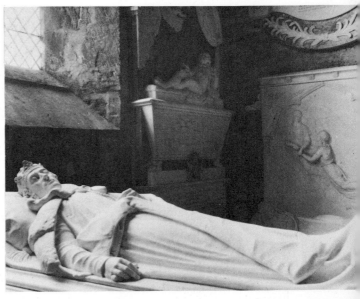

Above. Staindrop, St. Mary—fine medieval church with splendid tombs, the nearest by R. Westmacott 1842
Left. West Boldon, St. Nicholas. Spire mid 13th century
Below left. Ryton, Holy Cross. Lead covered spire 13th century

Although spires are rare, there are some fi examples. That at Darlington was rebuilt 1752, but the most elegant is at Chester-le-Stre c.1400. One interesting survival is the lea covered spire at Ryton, a type which also su mounted the west towers of Durham Cathed and the tower of Houghton-le-Spring until eighteenth century.

Apart from the magnificent bishops' tombs the Cathedral, the great families also produc their splendid monuments. The most impress are those of the Nevilles at Brancepeth a Staindrop, and a member of the Blakiston fan at Norton. The most curious is the series tombs at Chester-le-Street of 1594, some genu but many contrived to demonstrate the no lineage of Lord Lumley, back to the time Edward the Confessor! It is an intriguing ea example of medievalism.

Gothic Churches

23

CHESTER LE STREET,
St. Mary and St. Cuthbert

bove. Aisle of the tombs 1594

ght. The church is built on part of
e Roman site of Cunecastre. Its
gant spire—169 feet—c.1400 rises
ove an octagon and earlier tower

JOHN COSIN

Above and left. Egglescliffe, St. Mary. 15th-century church with robust Jacobean pews and a fine screen and fontcover

One of the most striking features of the churches in County Durham is the quality, variety and exuberance of post Reformation woodwork. Much of the medieval furnishing was destroyed at the Reformation although notable examples do survive at Staindrop, St. Andrew Auckland and at Durham Castle.

This new woodwork was the result of one man's work — John Cosin — who in 1662, became Bishop of Durham. He set out in the 1630's with a team of local craftsmen to replace the lost stalls, screens, etc., but in the manner and fashion of his day.

The earliest examples of his work include the strap work and balusters associated with the 'Jacobean' style and also, more unusually, Gothic ornament such as crockets, finials, pendants and poppy heads. Later the motifs changed towards the style of Wren and the Carolean school; putti, swags, and other ornament, often executed in a somewhat coarse but vigorous and lively way.

Brancepeth, St. Brandon. Woodwork c.1638 by Robert Barker

JOHN COSIN

Examples are too numerous to mention, but in addition to those illustrated there is work at Darlington, Aycliffe, Cockfield, St. Helen Auckland, the screens and stalls at Ryton and the font cover in Durham Cathedral. Secular woodwork in the same style, and executed by the same craftsmen exists at Durham Castle — the Black Stair (p.26) screens and doors — and in the Cosin Library. Cosin himself was a designer of some capability. The porch at Brancepeth Church and the restoration and conversion of the Chapel at Auckland Palace (p.51) are works for which he was directly responsible.

The tradition which Cosin established continued under Bishop Lord Crewe and was the beginning of a county reputation for fine woodwork which later produced many splendid staircases in Durham City.

Above. Haughton le Skerne, St. Andrew. Pulpit probably c.1660

Below left and right. Sedgefield, St. Edmund, naturalistic 13th-century capital and the c.1638 chancel fittings and screen

Aerial view showing the shell Keep and the Great Hall linked by the Galleries and Chapel

Kitchen 1499 with its early decorative brickwork

Black Stair 1662, inserted by John Cosi

Castles

BARNARD CASTLE AND WITTON

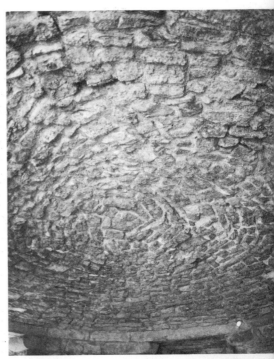

Above. Barnard Castle, Round Tower and west walls of the 14th century on Norman foundations
Above right. Flat domed vault of the Tower

Below. Witton Castle 1410, enlarged and altered in 1790 and the 19th century

The castle of the Prince Bishops at Durham was strategically the most important, but no-one interested in the functions and design of castles can afford to overlook the others in the county.

Although the present keep at Durham, on its great earth mound, is a conversion by Anthony Salvin in the nineteenth century, it gives a good idea of the form of the early shell keeps. These consisted originally of timber palisades surmounting the motte or hill and linked to the bailey or courtyard. Examples of these early castles survive throughout the north, as at Castle Hill, Bishopton. Naturally advantageous sites were chosen where they existed, as at Barnard Castle — rebuilt in stone after 1150 by Bernard Baliol, nephew of Guy de Baliol, to whom it had originally been granted by William Rufus.

HYLTON AND LUMLEY

Left. Hylton Castle c. 1400 is a fine example of a late castle. The windows were inserted in the 17th and 18th centuries when wings—since demolished —were added
Above. The 15th-century Hall, formerly the Chapel. The 18th-century doorcase is in the manner of James Gibbs

Lumley Castle, started c. 1300 was licensed in 1389 by the Bishop and in 1392 by the King. It is the most complete late castle in the county. Left. In the Great Hall, the elaborate fireplace inserted by John Lord Lumley in 1580

Right. Plasterwork by Francesco Vassali c. 1730 in the Garter Room Far right. Armorial shields of 1577 on the 14th century inner gateway

LUMLEY

View from the south. Basically a 15th-century stronghold, altered by John Patterson after 1817

19th-century 'chessmen' gatetowers

Castles grew as the importance of the holders developed, but it was not until the fourteenth century that compact and ordered plans like those of Lumley, Witton and Hylton were introduced. Lumley was built around a central courtyard with four great angle towers, and Hylton is a tall tower or keep without surrounding defences or bailey. These two were later transformed into houses, the former by Sir John Vanbrugh early in the eighteenth century.

Gradually, the defensive role became less necessary and gave way to the needs of more comfortable modes of living, although castles in the northern counties still had a military role to play until well into the seventeenth century. Some became country houses and were later extensively 'romanticised', as at Brancepeth. Others disappeared or became ruinous, like Ludworth Tower.

South west view. Centre sections 18th and 19th centuries. Park planted between 1727 and 1749

Below. East side, Chapel tower in centre altered in the 18th century

Raby is the epitome of the picturesque castle in a designed landscape. It was the seat until the sixteenth century of the most powerful family in the county, the Nevilles, who controlled and dominated much of south west County Durham. Although the building incorporates older sections, it is substantially a fourteenth century structure which started as a tower house, the main stronghold being at Brancepeth.

The pillared Lower Hall, originally built c.1325, was altered in 1782 by John Carr of York to become one of the first great dramatic Gothic Revival interiors. Other improvement schemes by him — and also James Paine — were only partly carried out, although Carr did design several estate buildings and farms.

Further alterations to the interior and south front by William Burns in the 1840's transformed it into a magnificent country house.

Lower Hall c.1325, altered 1782. Stairs inserted in 1864

Kitchen, 1378

Baron's Hall, timber roof by William Burn, 1844-1848

Ceiling of Octagon Room also by Bu

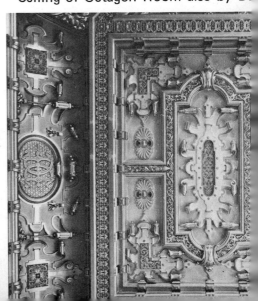

Manors

Although major estates were attached to the castles, defended dwellings such as Hollinside, Hunwick Hall and Bradley in Weardale formed the centres of other large land holdings. The pele tower, the traditional fortified refuge of the unsettled border lands, was often incorporated into later buildings, as at Hebburn Hall and Witton Tower.

After the turmoil and unrest of the middle ages, the seventeenth century at last brought the beginning of an age of prosperity, particularly in the fertile lands to the south and the good agricultural and sheep-rearing hill areas. Numerous manors and farmhouses were built as a result of this increased affluence and incorporated Renaissance details on doorways, fireplaces and stairs, although often the precise arrangement and design of this detailing was poorly understood. The best can stand comparison with similar houses in the Cotswolds and Derbyshire. But deep in the dales, people clung to the old traditions and methods of design—mullioned windows and decorated doorheads—right up to the end of the seventeenth century.

Above. Witton le Wear, Witton Tower. A pele refaced in the 17th century

Below and right. Stanhope Hall, a medieval house with unusual roof form, remodelled in the 16th and 17th centuries. Early windows in the gable

Washington Old Hall, built after 1613 on the site of an earlier house, the home of ancestors of George Washington—now restored

Above and left. Gainford Hall, entrance front, and panelling and plaster frieze in Great Hall, 1600

Below. Horden Hall, c.1600, a small complete manor house

Gainford Hall is probably the earliest of the formal houses of the seventeenth century. Building was started in 1600 by John Cradock, possibly with the advice of Robert Smythson—the builder of Hardwick Hall in Derbyshire. It was the first house in County Durham to be based on a square symmetrical plan and incorporates elaborate Renaissance detail around the main entrance even though the windows are still mullioned and transomed. It set a precedent for the county.

In the garden there is one of the large circular stone dovecots (p. 56) which were common to northern country houses as a source of winter meat.

Horden Hall is less compact and unusual in plan but the central porch is wider and even more elaborate with coupled Tuscan columns supporting a window bay.

Westholme near Winston 1607. Complete manor house of 'H' plan with a central hall

Thornton Hall, 17th century, sash windows 18th century   West Auckland Hall. Altered 1670

Above. New Holmside Hall 1668 with early 18th-century extensions. About to be demolished

Right, above and below. Esh Hall, window detail 1687 and 17th-century gate pier with open scrolled finial

Below. Stanhope, Unthank Hall, a 17th-century house with unusual three shaft chimney, windows later

Right. Ireshopeburn, Newhouse 17th century. The tall windows still with hood moulds—see New Holmside, p.37. Behind is a large barn-like building erected by W. B. Beaumont M.P. as a library and news room for local miners

Below. Tanfield Hall, an early house refronted in the 18th century. The ironwork is the finest in the county

Above. Durham City, Crook Hall. A complete medieval manor house with hall and screens passage (far right) extended in 1671. The three storey brick wing is Georgian

Below. West Boldon Hall, early house refaced 1709

Below. Fencehouses, Morton Hall, 1709

Above. School Aycliffe, elegant Georgian villa c.1790
Left. Headlam Hall, Jacobean house refronted in the
18th century

The main characteristics of much eighteenth century architecture are:— simple rectangular compositions, severe classical cornices and pediments, the minimum of decoration and well-proportioned Georgian windows with sash bars. In the more elaborate designs these were surrounded and surmounted by correct classical mouldings, but in the simpler farms and manor houses they had plain stone architraves. It was a respectable architecture, dignified but unpretentious.

Left. Felling, Crow Hall, orderly Georgian stone house
Below. Gainford, White Cross. Planned 18th-century
farmstead

terlee, Shotton Hall c.1780. Bow windows and ironwork added later. Now Peterlee Development
rporation Offices

hitburn, startling Victorian decoration
69

Sunderland, Tunstall Lodge c.1840. Elegant house of
stucco, wide eaves and Grecian porch.

WALWORTH CASTLE c.1600

Above. View from the south showing the interesting angle towers. James 1 of England stayed here in 1603
Left. Spectacular entrance porch of three stages of classical orders — Tuscan, Ionic and Corinthian

Right. Biddick Hall c.1723, in the manner of Vanbrugh who stayed at nearby Lumley Castle in 1721

The great houses of County Durham are relatively modest and do not rival the splendours of Castle Howard in Yorkshire or Mellerstain in Roxburghshire. Some are adapted castles and there are a few seventeenth century houses which show the characteristics of rather belated early Renaissance architecture in England. The lordly style of Sir John Vanbrugh and Nicholas Hawksmore (sometimes called English Baroque) appears in the re-modelling of Lumley Castle and is echoed in such houses as Biddick Hall, but the best age of house building in Durham was after the middle of the eighteenth century and the Palladian style, made popular by Lord Burlington, seems to have appealed particularly to northern landowners.

THE HALL, ST. HELEN AUCKLAND

Above. The small Drawing Room. The panels are possibly from Streatlam Castle, c. 1868

Above. The chaste 18th century Palladian wing
Below left. Rococo ceiling in the Saloon

James Paine, whose practice started in Yorkshire, was perhaps the most widely approved architect and he designed many great houses in the northern counties. Among these were Bradley Hall, Axwell Park, Coxhoe Hall (now demolished), the landscape buildings of Hardwick Hall and the elegant chapel at Gibside overlooking the Derwent. A number of smaller houses were rebuilt to conform with the fashion set by Paine. Though successful architects from the south, such as Gibbs, Campbell and Sir Thomas Robinson, are represented, the majority of buildings in the county were the work of local men who established a strong tradition in the area.

Imported talents during the eighteenth century gradually changed the taste and fashion of interior design. Itinerant Italian craftsmen executed decorative plasterwork of high quality at Auckland Palace and the houses at Croxdale, Elemore and St. Helen Auckland.

...more Hall. Mid 18th-century brick house with stone ...essings, containing fine plasterwork in the manner of ...useppe Cortese

Darlington, Blackwell Grange 1700 later additions of 1722 and 1900

...ubb House near Winston, central wing 1750 and ...vilions 1816 added to an earlier house of 1690

Croxdale Hall, staircase ceiling 18th century, possibly by Cortese

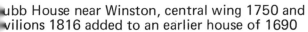

GIBSIDE

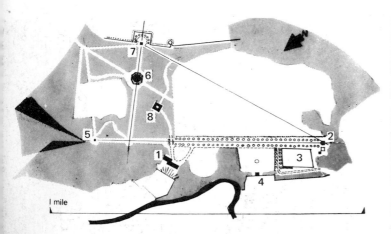

Key to plan:—

1. Hall
2. Mausoleum, later the Chapel
3. Walled Garden
4. Orangery
5. Column of British Liberty
6. Fishpond
7. Banqueting House
8. Stable Block

Gibside is the most complete remaining example of a landscape garden in the county. It was created between 1729 and 1760 to the design of its owner George Bowes. The house of 1625 was altered in the 19th century, but the landscape buildings are possibly by James Paine and erected between 1750-60. The Chapel, the finest of the buildings and certainly by Paine was completed in 1812

Above. Porch of the Hall 1625

Below left. Stable Block c.1750

Below. Gothick Banqueting House

GIBSIDE CHAPEL

Above.
The Chapel
from the
Avenue

Left.
Plasterwork
in dome

Right.
Column of
British Liberty
from the
Chapel

Axwell Park, 1758 by James Paine, illustrated in his *Plans Elevations and Sections of Noblemen and Gentlemen's Houses . . .* 1767. The interior was much altered in the 19th century

Hardwick Hall, roof structure of The Temple 1754—57, now derelict. Probably designed by James Paine

Axwell Park, Dower House, a Gothi villa of c.1770—1780

HAMSTERLEY HALL

The Gothick house c.1770 — a genial mixture of elements from different places and periods. The pinnacle is from the old Houses of Parliament and the cupola (right) from Beaudesert, Staffordshire

Left. Georgian Gothick at its happiest

Though Palladian architecture is well represented with fine examples at Gibside Chapel (p.47) and Axwell Park nostalgia for the stirring history of the county seems to have fostered a taste for 'Gothick' architecture and decoration.

Thus, from about 1750, Gothick architecture in the fashion set by Horace Walpole at Strawberry Hill, Middlesex, gained many adherents in the north. This new Gothick was a light-hearted decorative style, endearing in its cheerful disregard of the nature of true Gothic building, and in the ingenuity and playfulness of the results.

The Hall, late 18th century. Rebuilt about 1820
by Rowland Burdon, possibly with the advice of
Sir John Soane

Below. Gothic lodge 1800 by
William Atkinson of Auckland

After about 1790, the light-hearted rococo
Gothick was succeeded by a more serious revival
of Gothic architecture, giving rise to severe and
pretentious castellated designs of which Brancepeth and Raby (pp. 30,31) are good examples;
the former being very grand and baronial, the
latter almost teutonic. One of the most picturesque
new castles was Ravensworth, at the south end
of the Team Valley Trading Estate. This was
John Nash's only work in the north, but collapsed
due to mining subsidence and has now been
demolished.

Many of the great houses have Gothic features
on the estate. These provided a whimsical and
often welcome relief to the sobriety of the
Palladian mansions they accompanied.

Great Houses

AUCKLAND PALACE

Auckland Palace has been the residence of the Bishops of Durham since the twelfth century. The buildings form a loosely linked group dating from these earlier times, but superficially are of the seventeenth and eighteenth centuries.

The most important part of the group is Bishop Pudsey's Great Hall (twelfth century) which was converted, furnished and externally refaced by Bishop Cosin after 1660 to form the Chapel. Tall, light and airy, with robust and elaborate fittings and furnishings, it is one of the most splendid chapels in England.

The series of State Rooms, though medieval in structure, were decorated and Gothicised in the late eighteenth century by James Wyatt. He also designed the fine screen wall and inner gateway.

The elegant and amusing gateway to the town was probably designed by Richard Bentley, a member of Horace Walpole's 'Strawberry Hill' Committee of Taste.

Auckland Palace sits close to the centre of Bishop Auckland, with a mature landscape park on its other side. This contains the curious, cloister-like Deer House (p.57).

Above and below. The Chapel interior and Cosin's elaborate ceiling of c.1660

The exterior of the Chapel showing the geometric refacing and later clerestorey

Entrance
screen by
James Wyatt
c.1795

Left.
Doorway in
Great Room
remodelled
c.1795

Right.
Charles I
Room, rococo
plaster ceiling,
mid 18th
century

Great Houses

BEAMISH AND WYNYARD PARK

The early nineteenth century saw the revival of classical design with strong influence from Greece, and the north participated at a very early stage in the Greek revival. Ignatius Bonomi of Durham and John Dobson of Newcastle both practised in the Greek manner with considerable distinction. They were also capable, as was customary at the time, of turning their hand to designing in any other style of architecture.

Left. Beamish Hall, a house of 1737, extended and enlarged in 1813, 1897, and 1909. Now the centre of the Open Air Museum

Below. Wynyard Park, begun in 1822 for the third Marquess of Londonderry by Phillip Wyatt, fourth son of James Wyatt. It was gutted by fire in 1841 and rebuilt by Phillip Wyatt and Ignatius Bonomi

Great Houses

LAMBTON CASTLE

Page 54.
Above. Burn Hall, 1821-34 to the design of Ignatius
Bonomi, built by Moody — the Ushaw builder
Below, left and right. Windlestone Hall, 1834 also
by Bonomi — the long arcaded loggia front and
stable clock tower

Lambton Castle. A picturesque house which is the
product of several rebuildings — the first between
1798 and 1801 by Joseph Bonomi, and later in 1862
by Sidney Smirke and John Dobson. In the 1930's
the house was reduced in size.
   The grounds contain fine bridges, a stable block
and an interesting Neo-Norman chapel of c.1840

Right. House from main terrace showing the flying
buttresses
Below left. Porte Cochère and main entrance
Below right. Romantic tower — now detached

Bedburn, Hoppyland Hall, lodge in cottage ornée style

Gate lodges, stables and other buildings associated with great houses often reflect the quality and aspiration of the house. They set the scene for the principal building but sometimes provide a direct contrast as at Raby. They are occasionally the only remnant of a departed great house like Streatlam Castle, the home of the Bowes who built their own Museum at Barnard Castle (p. 82).

Gainford Hall, 17th-century dovecot

Witton Castle, dovecot and prospect tower, late 18th century

Brancepeth, estate vernacular in main village street

Estate Buildings

Above and below. Raby Castle, Georgian Gothick pavilion c.1775 and the 18th-century Palladian stables

Auckland Palace, cloister-like Gothick deer house 1760 Below. Ushaw College, Home Farm — the powerful farm buildings by John Hansom, 1851-52

Chester le Street, 14th-century horse-shoe arched bridge over the Wear near Lambton Park

Below. Winch Bridge, rebuilt after
a disaster in 1820

River crossings over Tees, Wear and Tyne have been important in the history and development of the county. The thirteenth century Sunderland Bridge at Croxdale, the County Bridge at Barnard Castle and Bishop Skirlaw's bridge over the Tees at Yarm are important early examples.

The need to improve communications in the eighteenth century produced many more. Winston Bridge — designed by the accomplished amateur architect Sir Thomas Robinson, Abbey Bridge near Egglestone Abbey and Prebends Bridge in Durham are elegant and handsome Georgian structures.

Constructional experiments produced the Winch Bridge, Teesdale, built for leadminers in 1744. It is perhaps the earliest of all metal suspension bridges. The larger Whorlton Suspension Bridge was built only nine years after Sir Samuel Brown's pioneer work culminated in the Union Bridge over the Tweed in 1820. Meanwhile, cast iron had been successfully used at Sunderland for the first bridge of 1793.

The bridges which today are most evident are those associated with the railway mania of the last century. No valley seemed too broad to span with great viaducts, often elegant and always impressive. They show northern engineering genius at its best. There are too many to list here, but the Victoria Viaduct at Washington, the tall viaduct at Hounsgill and the sophisticated brick structure at Thorpe Thewles are worthy of special mention.

The Tanfield or Causey Arch near Stanley was the work of a local mason, Ralph Wood, in 1729. Built to carry the coal waggonway, it may perhaps be the earliest of all 'railway' bridges.

Left. The single leap of the Causey Arch 1729 by Ralph Wood, a local mason

Below left. Thorpe Thewles, the elegant early 19th-century railway viaduct — engineers' architecture at its best

Below. Consett, Hounsgill Viaduct, a finely detailed structure of 1856, designed by Sir Thomas Bouch

The survival or revival of pre-Reformation modes of design lasted through the seventeenth century, first with Bishop Cosin's splendid woodwork—a conscious mixture of the style of his own day with the Gothic past—and secondly in the only complete seventeenth century church in the county, St. Mary le Bow, Durham (1685).

The eighteenth century growth of trade and prosperity saw the development and enlargement of the county's ports. Stockton replaced Yarm on the Tees and the growing towns of Sunderland and South Shields required new churches. But generally the eighteenth century was not an age of church building; houses and domestic comfort had priority. Visits of John Wesley, preaching at St. John, Sunderland in 1784 and throughout the county, encouraged non-conformity which was to become very strong in Victorian Durham. No village or hamlet was too small to have its little and sometimes great chapel, particularly among the leadmining communities where non-conformity is still strong.

The Parish Church at Stockton was built in 1710-12 with the advice of Sir Christopher Wren. The chancel and chapels were added or rebuilt much later. Sunderland has two Georgian churches; the principal one, the parish church of Holy Trinity, was built in 1719 and enlarged with a curious circular apse in 1735. The other is St. John.

Above left. Gateshead, St. Mary, remodelled in the 18th century. West tower of 1740, upper stages c.177
Left. Stockton, the Parish Church, 1710-12, west towe
Page 61.
Left. Sunderland, Holy Trinity 1719. Interior looking west
Above right. St. John's Chapel, Parish Church, 1752
Below right. Castle Eden, St. James, 1764

Above. South Shields, St. Hilda
c.1768. The galleries and columns
were inserted in 1810-11

Right. West Hartlepool, Christ Church
1854 by E. B. Lamb. A large and
highly unusual church for one of the
newly emergent towns

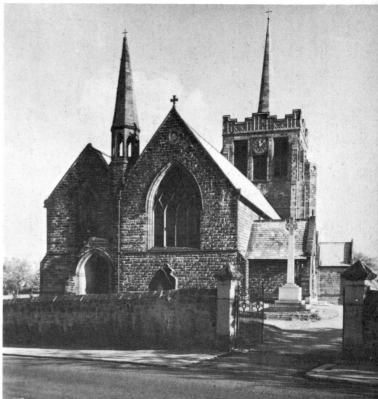

bove. Hunstanworth, St. James 1863
S. S. Teulon

Above. Stanley, St. Thomas 1876 by J. G. Holl,
enlarged and tower added 1931
Below left. Sunderland, Christ Church, Victorian
stained glass window in the south aisle

The nineteenth century, in County Durham as in the rest of England, was an age of enormous change, movement of population and growth of towns and cities. New churches were needed almost everywhere and the new colliery villages and towns had to make do, as a rule, with cheap and simple buildings. However, they are often the principal buildings of merit in a town or village and much of the character and quality of these places depends on them in terms of townscape, skyline and general interest.

The grander churches tended to be in the expanding towns and some of these, like Christ Church, Hartlepool (by E. B. Lamb) are monuments to the exuberant confidence, if not perversity of the age.

West Hartlepool, Methodist Church 1871-73, a large and grand example

Methodist, Unitarian, Baptist churches and Friends' meeting houses are important buildings throughout the county. Early examples are handsome brick structures with classical ornament. Later chapels are usually stone-built, and although classical motifs were used until the 1870's, by 1850 Gothic details and plan forms were the rule.

The church of St. Andrew, Roker, is outstanding. It is the work of one of Victorian England's 'rogue' architects, E. S. Prior. Perhaps equally outstanding is the team of craftsmen he assembled to complete the building—Ernest Gimson, designer and cabinet maker, Morris and Company who provided carpets and wove the great tapestry, and the young Eric Gill, who cut the inscriptions. It is one of the finest products of the Arts and Crafts movement.

Stockton, Baptist Tabernacle 1904, a hybrid of many styles in startling materials

Below and right. Roker, St. Andrew 1906-7 by E. S. Prior. Tower and chancel of local grey limestone, and the powerful interior like a great inverted boat

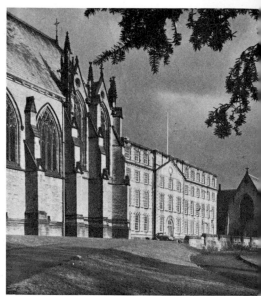

Above. Original block (centre) 1803-1
and main chapel detailing (left)

The Chapel interior 1885 by Dunn and Hansom

Chapel of St. Charles Borromeo 1857
by E. W. Pugin

The buildings of the College at Ushaw were
started in 1803 with the orderly pedimented
central block; the top storey was added later.
Subsequent buildings were designed by Dunn and
Hansom, Edward Pugin and his father A. W. N.
Pugin—the passionate protagonist of the truth
and order of Gothic architecture and designer of
the detail and ornament on the Palace of Westminster. The magnificent detailing of the Chapel
of St. Charles Borromeo serves to show that
craftsmen of 1857 could rival in virtuosity those
of medieval England.

BISHOP AUCKLAND

The large towns of the county, like Gateshead and South Shields, have their roots in antiquity but today they present a predominantly industrial picture. Some, like West Hartlepool and Seaham Harbour, are the result of conscious nineteenth century effort to plan industrial communities, whilst others such as Stockton, Bishop Auckland, and the large village-towns of Sedgefield and Wolsingham, are based upon ancient market centres.

Some of the towns had been fortified. Stretches of the medieval walls of Durham City and parts of the walls and Town Gate at Hartlepool (p. 77) remain as isolated fragments of defence works.

The speed, scale and recklessness of nineteenth and twentieth century building has in many cases obscured the earlier form of the towns. They now remain in plan only and in small pockets such as the remnants of 'village' greens.

Areas of large Victorian and Edwardian residential building close to the centres of several towns are architecturally attractive — the leafy Victorian suburbia of Ashbrooke at Sunderland, the areas immediately south and west of Darlington and to the west of the Hartlepools.

The most visually satisfying towns are those like Barnard Castle where a limited range of building material gives harmony and unity; nevertheless there is great interest and entertainment in the varied styles and brash juxtaposition within the Victorian streets of Durham towns.

Above left. Gatehouse to the Bishop's Palace from the Market Place, 1760, probably by Richard Bentley, a friend of Horace Walpole. Castle Lodge (to the right) 17th century

Left. Newgate Street, an amusing baronial bank building of 1859

SUNDERLAND

Above. High Street East, shopfront c.185
Left. The Empire Theatre 1906 by W. and
T.R. Milburn and the Dun Cow Inn, both
Edwardian Baroque
Below left. High Street, 'Hindoo Gothic'
1873-77
Below. Fire Station 1906-7

The Esplanade, Victorian terrace housing of c.1860, still in the Georgian tradition. It is the best of many similar terraces thoughout the town

Merchant Seamen's Almshouses, Trafalgar Square, 1840

Langham Tower, an industrialist's mansion of 1885 in the Neo-Tudor style

SOUTH SHIELDS

Above and right. Town Hall 1903 by E.E. Fetch.
The most splendid civic building in the county
Below. Old Town Hall in the Market Place, 1768

WESTOE AND NORTON

Westoe, village now part of South Shields. Georgian Gothick and Classical houses

Norton, fine 18th and early 19th-century houses flanking the tree lined High Street

STOCKTON ON TEES

Above. Town Hall 1736, the centre of the long wide High Street
Above left. Church Street, fine Georgian houses
Left. 72 Paradise Row, elaborate doorcase c.1730
Below. Victorian terrace housing, typical of the industrial towns of the county—plain and honest

Towns and Villages

HOUGHTON LE SPRING

Kepier Grammar School, founded 1574, extended
1724 and 1779
The Old Hall, the manor house of the village c.1600

Davenport Almshouses 1668

Medieval Rectory, now U.D.C. Offices

Above. Londonderry Institute, opened 1855, designed by Thomas Oliver. The layout for the new harbour and town was prepared by John Dobson between 1823 and 1828. Little materialised and even less remains

Right. Gateshead, Walker Terrace, c. 1830, an elegant group of houses set on rising ground

bove. Town Hall 1868, detail showing
ueen Victoria and the cast iron clock-
ittle Big Ben'
ight. Saltwell Towers c.1860. Romantic
airytale castle', built for W. Wailes, the
orthern stained glass artist
elow. Shipley Art Gallery 1915 —
arnest neo-classicism

Left.
North Road
Station,
1842

Right.
Tower and
Market Hall,
1864 by
Alfred
Waterhouse

Left.
Bank in
High Row,
1864, also
by Alfred
Waterhouse

Right.
Bank Top
Station,
Clock Tower
1887 by
William Bell
architect to
the North
East Railway

DARLINGTON AND HARTLEPOOL

Above left and right. Darlington. Regency houses — Coniscliffe Road and Harewood Grove, some of the best in the county

Left and below. Hartlepool. Georgian houses facing the harbour, and the medieval Sandwell Gate

Left.
'The Shades'
Inn, detail of
Art Nouveau
ironwork and
terra cotta
c.1900

Above right.
Dock Offices
c.1853

Right.
Original Custom
House 1844

Left.
Municipal
Buildings 1889,
terra cotta
detailing

Below right.
Grand Hotel
1889 by
J. Garry

Above. Hallgarth Street, medieval Tithe Barn of the Priory
Above left. Kepier Hospital, the 1341 Gateway built by Bishop Bury
Below. Saddler Street, a medieval way. Foreground, the surviving pay box to the Georgian theatre

Durham City is unique in Britain and almost so in western Europe. The city is a visual complement and foil to the buildings on the rock. In reality, it is three towns, or rather three clear phases of development. The medieval citadel of Cathedral, Castle and buildings on the peninsula; the county town of elegant eighteenth century houses in the Elvets and the Baileys; and the nineteenth century town promoted by the railways to function as a focal point for the coalfield. It is a city centred on a strong nucleus of peninsula and market place and is linked by two medieval bridges to the radiating spurs of development in the deep wooded valleys. Throughout its past, its role as administrative centre of the county has produced fine buildings like Bonomi's Assize Courts; the University — established by Bishop Van Mildert in 1833 — has produced and continues to produce interesting buildings which contribute to the drama and excitement of the City.

Above. College Green. Behind the octagonal Conduit House of 1751 stands the early 19th-century Registry, both Gothic Revival
Left. The splendid early 18th-century doorcase of Cosin's Hall
Below. 18th and early 19th-century houses in Old Elvet

DURHAM CITY

Above. Assize Courts 1809-11 started by Francis Sandys and completed by Ignatius Bonomi

Above left. Market Place, Georgian and Victorian houses and shops. In foreground, statue of the Marquess of Londonderry 1861 by R. Monti

Left. Town Hall, interior by Phillip C. Hardwick, 1851. This splendid hall with its timber hammer beam roof is based on the design of that at Westminster Hall

BARNARD CASTLE

Above. The Market Cross and Town Hall 1747, an unusual combination of open market with an octagonal hall above
Above left. The Bank, Blagroves House, 16th century
Left. Barnard Castle School 1886, by Clark and Moscrop of Darlington. Chapel 1910 by W. D. Caroe

Page 82. Bowes Museum, begun in 1869 by Jules Pellechet

Initially, the prosperity based upon the exploitation of coal and iron led to the building of great Victorian villas, but increasingly and unhappily, as the blight of industry spread, wealthy landowners made their homes elsewhere.

During the nineteenth century many architects believed that they could draw upon all the best architecture of the past for example and inspiration. This was called eclecticism and as a result, there is a wide variety of style of which perhaps the most astounding is the great French Renaissance chateau museum built by John and Josephine Bowes at Barnard Castle.

Above. Sedgefield. Manor House, a stately 18th century building. Now U.D.C. Offices

Above. Sedgefield. Houses of local brick and pantile, the traditional materials in this large lowland village

Below. West Auckland. Elegant early 19th-century bowed shop front

The older villages of the county, the variety and interest of their plans and the quality of their buildings deserve much more space than can be provided here. They take several forms; long street villages of brick and pantile along the gentler stretches of the Tees, villages of stone with a series of streets radiating from a central point or market place, or, the most interesting of all, those like West Auckland and Staindrop bordering a series of large and spacious interlocking greens. Often the size and arrangement of these greens was determined by factors associated with the defence of the village, rather in the way the wagon trains of the 'western' epic were formed for defence.

Durham villages show a rich variety of settlement pattern and many of those developed in the eighteenth century are very charming with their simple and varied Georgian buildings.

GAINFORD AND STAINDROP

inford. High Row, Georgian houses and cottages—stucco and pantile—in an attractive Teesdale village

indrop. Stone village near Raby Castle with an interesting plan of interconnecting greens

Above. Hurworth. Manor House, 1728 (now a preparatory school)

Above. Hurworth, early Victorian Gothic cottages fronting the main street
Left. Middleton in Teesdale. Masterman Place, archway and housing probably designed by Ignatius Bonomi c.1845

Improved communications brought better understanding of classical forms and famous architects such as Sir John Vanbrugh came to work in the north. Under this classical influence a rich and varied regional style of vernacular architecture was evolved with characteristic local variations. It lasted until the 1850's. The standard type of five bay house, of two or three floors, wide, tall and handsome, became the aspiration of all those who prospered from trade and the benefits of the agricultural revolution. Examples exist in almost every village of consequence, Whickham, West Boldon, Wolsingham, Heighington, the Aucklands and many others.

Above. Middleton One Row
Above right. Egglescliffe, 18th-century
cottages round a green
Right and below right. Heighington,
a spacious village green, and one of the
fine 18th-century houses
Below. Witton le Wear, 19th-century
village houses in Station Road

Above. Ryton, mid-18th century house with Venetian windows
Above right. Wolsingham, Whitfield Place 1677, and Whitfield House (left) c.1700
Right. High Coniscliffe, 18th-century houses in the main street
Below right. Hamsterley, Georgian Baptist Chapel
Below. Whickham, cottage conversion from a Georgian Gothick archway

Above. Oakenshaw, trim colliery housing — pairs formed into a long row

In the mining areas, the villages were naturally related to the workings and the industrial scene which is still part and parcel of the environment. The cottages were characteristically built in rows, presenting the minimum of external wall area and keeping each other warm by nestling together, in sheltered valleys wherever possible.

Coal mining — the seed of nineteenth century industry — began commercially in the seventeenth century, but the nineteenth century reaped the effects. Agricultural villages were now joined by new industrial communities growing alongside, and settlements sprouted wherever mining was profitable. Towns and villages, based on lead mining in the highlands, shrank as coal mining in the east drew people away to new or expanding industrial towns.

Though pitmen's cottages, frequently built of brick — a by-product of the collieries — were simple and economical in construction, one needs to remember that, in their day, they often provided improved standards of accommodation and sanitation. Also, they began as a single row with country all around and the monotony which would result from repetition of such rows on a large scale was not originally envisaged. Nineteenth century housing and planning was often more enlightened than modern prejudices allow people to admit; witness the pioneer layout and design of Tudhoe Grange by the Salvin family in 1865.

Behind the disfigurements of advertisement, power lines and industrial waste, these homes show — more than any other type of housing — the history of a hard-working, tightly-knit community in cottages of considerable character.

Centre and left. Cold Hesledon, unusual and decorative brick terrace housing, double and single storied — 'cottage' housing is common in the county and particularly in Sunderland

Weardale, Killhope, the lead crushing mill, a majestic relic of lead mining days

Castle Eden. Cotton Mill now Brewery, late 18th century

Bedburn Mill, completed before 1820

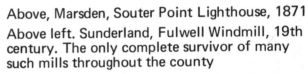

Above, Marsden, Souter Point Lighthouse, 1871

Above left. Sunderland, Fulwell Windmill, 19th century. The only complete survivor of many such mills throughout the county

Below left. South Shields, navigational leading marks at the entry to the River Tyne, in the form of obelisks, c. 1810

Below. Seaham Harbour, harbour and coal staithes 1828, for the new town and port built by the third Marquess of Londonderry

Durham City, Observatory meridian 1850

Westerton, Wright's Observatory c. 1785

Penshaw Monument, to the first Earl of Durham, 1844

Blaydon, Summer house c. 1760, associated with Stella Hall now demolished

Above. Westernhopeburn, a long low stone house of 1606

Above right. Stotley Hall, 17th-century farmhouse

Right. Esh Hall. A magnificent 17th-century barn interior of timber and stone construction

Vernacular building — the long slow development of a traditional architecture through applied good sense and a respect for materials — is rich and varied in the county. It reflects not only local variations of natural materials, such as stone, but also the effects of trade and industry in the production and use of brick and pantile, initially imported from the Low Countries.

Settlement patterns vary not only between highland and lowland regions but also from north to south, the main dividing line being where the 'burns' of the north become the 'becks' of the south.

It is impossible here to indicate the range and variety of vernacular design as each little region can provide opportunities for fascinating study of local building traditions.

94.
Top. Little Causey Farm near Beamish
Centre left. Farm buildings at Headlam — Teesdale
Whitewash and pantile
Centre right. Stone and pantile at Hamsterley. Note
the courses of stone at the eaves — a Yorkshire and
Durham traditional detail
Below left. Barn at Middle End Farm, Teesdale
Below right. Cottages at West Auckland

Above. Moorland cottages, Tunstall
House, Weardale
Below left. Upland stone detailing,
St. John's Chapel. Low pitched
graded stone slab roof
Below right. Westgate, Polly's Cottage.
Like many highland dwellings the roof
'catslides' to near ground level at the
rear

Above. Beamish, Shepherd and Shepherdess Inn. The fine lead figures are 18th century

Right. Egglescliffe, lowland vernacular of brick and pantile

Below right. Mid Durham farm at West Edmondsley. Door dated 1751

Below. Hunwick Old Hall, farm 'gin' or engine house for a horse driven machine

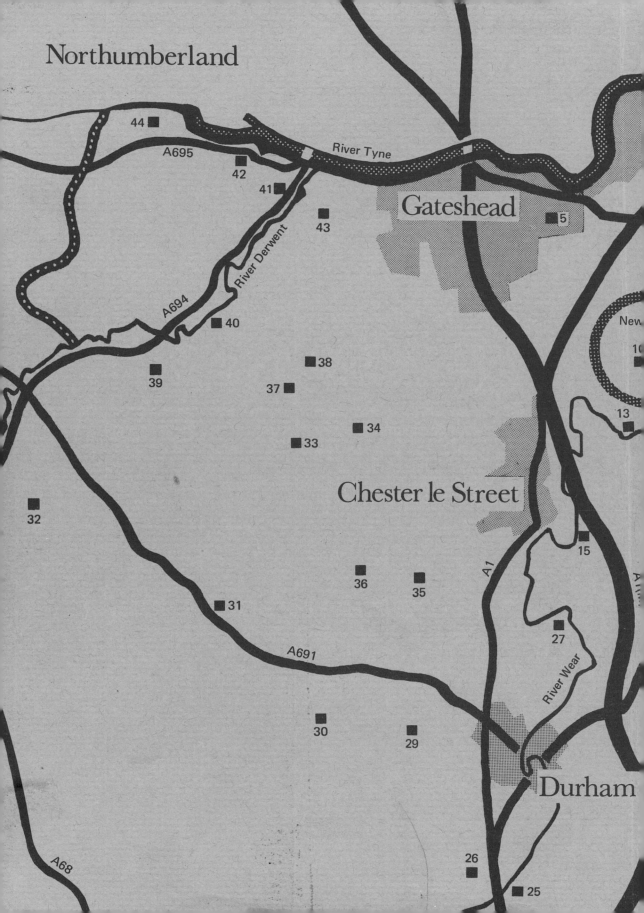